# LOVING HER LIKE HIM

Charleston, SC
www.PalmettoPublishing.com

*Loving Her Like Him*
Copyright © 2022 by Tyler Frazier

All Scripture references in this book are taken from the King James Version.

First Edition

ISBN: 978-1-63837-939-3

# Loving Her Like Him

TYLER FRAZIER

# The Origin

Welcome to my story. I'm glad to have you! It is safe to assume you purchased this book because you desired a greater revelation of *love*—well, so did I. So get comfortable as I share with you what the Lord gave me, but first allow me to share with you the origins of this book, which I hope will prompt you to read further.

The material in this book was not acquired easily. It was birthed out of extreme love, passion, and pain. It was my love for a woman paired with a passion burning with vehement intensity and the pain of the thought of failing. For a long time, I've been preparing for my wife, marinating in the seasoning of excitement for a woman I have not met yet and eager to provide her with the optimum marriage experience as my gift to her. "Optimum" means reaching the highest potential that is or can ever be obtained by a thing. It is experiencing the full benefits of everything available. You see, I am an extremist. When I set my mind on something dear to my heart, I will go to great lengths to achieve it. In certain cases, I can be so extreme that people have called me downright crazy. In this situation, I was crazy…crazy in love. I wanted to make sure I would be an awesome husband who would give her the greatest marriage. There would be no settling, and she wouldn't be hurt because of my lack of knowledge about marriage. An optimum marriage was the goal—if that didn't happen, I certainly didn't want it to be my fault.

The current divorce rate in the United States is almost 50 percent, and it is surprisingly much higher in other countries! If that's not troubling enough, it is said that of the remaining 50 percent of married couples, the vast majority are unhappily married (it's complicated to quantify happiness). Honestly, those numbers scared me. Nobody goes into a marriage planning to experience pain or heartache or get a divorce. However, divorce happens to an astronomical number of people—really good people. I didn't want this to be our case. I love her too much.

With all this in mind, I decided in my heart to read, search out, and study all I could find pertaining to marriage. Remember, this is an extremist talking. In any field, the people you find who are extraordinary at what they do spend years studying and learning their craft. Let's consider the legendary Michael

Jordan, who was great because, along with his athletic talent, he knew the game of basketball backward and forward. You will find that he spent most of his days watching and studying tapes, learning what to do, what not to do, what worked, and what didn't. The same can be said of Bill Gates, who spent days at a time writing code. So I began my research years before I thought I was ready to become a husband. I started collecting tapes, CDs, literature, and so forth and quickly discovered most teachings on marriage would often reference the Bible and scripture. This made sense because the origin of marriage came from God and the first documented marriage is in the Bible. As my quest continued, I focused my search on God and what the Bible had to say about marriage. To my surprise, I uncovered insights that I never imagined would be revealed to me.

What you are about to read did not come from me. I take no credit for it; I'm just not that intelligent. The knowledge in this book came from God. If you don't believe in God, certainly you believe in love, so I encourage you to still read the book and judge the content. You will benefit from the material within it. If you are married, plan on getting married, or are just in love, continue reading.

# CHAPTER 1

# Marriage Is a Mystery

Ephesians 5:31–32 reads as follows: "For this cause shall a man leave his father and mother, and shall be joined unto his wife, and they two shall be one flesh. This is a great mystery."

Listen, the first thing one must know is this: marriage is a mystery! Not only is it a mystery, but the scripture plainly says it is a great mystery. The superlative "great" speaks of something beyond ordinary and something massive, something with humongous potential and enormous benefits. There is a difference between an ordinary piece of artwork and a masterpiece; marriage is a mysterious masterpiece, which is why so many end in divorce. So let's go back to the fact shared above and question why nearly 50 percent of marriages don't end up working out. We should first start by acknowledging that 100 percent of people go into marriage not even knowing it's a mystery. And guess what happens? Because it's a mystery, they try it for a while—a year, two years, fifteen years—and then they realize *they can't figure it out*. The divorce rate simply reflects the majority who have said, "This mystery is too hard," and they call it quits. I like to say marriage is a five-thousand-piece puzzle. For those who divorce, it doesn't mean they are bad, wrong, or incapable. It just means the "puzzle" got the best of them.

For those who stay married, this doesn't necessarily mean they solved the mystery. Based on my studies, there seem to be two paths for these couples. It either means they are two amazingly strong and determined individuals whose love runs so deep that they choose to remain married, or they are doing the best they can and don't want other people to know they couldn't solve the mystery, so they just stick it out. The latter couple described, although they are still married, have typically given up and yet will remain together, sitting in an unsolved puzzle. As the marriage vow goes, "Till death do us part." One would agree that those "sticking it out" aren't obtaining the full potential and benefits of marriage. How can they reap the full benefits of viewing a masterpiece if the painting is not yet finished? Most people are looking at an unfinished picture of the masterpiece of marriage that God designed.

Back to the puzzle, the key to solving any puzzle is to first behold the original image. Having this knowledge empowers you because it would otherwise be challenging to piece together something you have never seen before. Without the original image, the mystery is beyond impossible to solve. This causes one to question why God would give us this wonderful masterpiece and then make it a mystery to solve? It doesn't make sense that God would want to keep us from experiencing *all* of something as wonderful and natural as marriage.

Why would He hide something so great from us? Or is He hiding something so great *for* us?

# CHAPTER 2

# Mysteries and Secrets Revealed

In my studies, it was plain to me that the origin of marriage started with God. That said, why would He make it so extremely hard for us to understand marriage, which He intended to be so great?

This is a hard question that I pondered for some time until I came across a scripture in the Bible.

Amazingly, I found that Jesus's disciples had a similar question. During his time on earth, Jesus often spoke in parables or riddles, making it hard for people to understand the things he was saying. One day, his disciples asked, "Why do you speak to the crowds in parables?" They were simply asking him, "Why are you hiding things from us and speaking in secret?"

Matthew 13:11 says, "He answered and said unto them, Because it is given unto *you* to know the mysteries of the kingdom of heaven, but to them it is not given [emphasis mine]."

When I reflected on the scripture above, it was like a light bulb came on and God allowed me inside his head, sharing with me his thoughts and purpose in doing this. In this particular scripture, Jesus was speaking to his disciples (those who believed in him), not to those in the crowd who did not believe. Paraphrasing, Jesus was saying the mysteries of life and heaven are not given to everyone but are for those who believe and seek him. Another scripture confirms this—"He who comes to God must believe that he exists and that he is a rewarder of them that diligently seek him" (Hebrews 11:6). You see, there are benefits and rewards that God has for those who seek him—wonderful rewards that will exponentially bless your life, one of which is an optimal marriage experience!

How can you expect to fully partake in something that originated in heaven and is so great (marriage) yet not believe in or seek after the God who created it? It's as if God is saying, "I created marriage, and therefore only I fully understand how to make it work. If you want to completely understand this mystery, then you must come to me to learn the secret." Many people are trying to do what God created without God. The result of trying to make something work without consulting with the person who created it is exactly what we have in most marriages today: a stalemate.

After God made the first humans, Adam and Eve, his next creation was marriage. This is the first and oldest institution, which is why it is natural for human beings to desire mates. God, in his infinite wisdom, created this wonderful mystery and put it in place, knowing that humans would have no choice but to seek him out to enjoy and understand this magnificent mystery! Those who humble themselves, realize they need help, and seek him will be rewarded. Those who either don't believe or simply refuse to seek God will never in this lifetime behold or experience the complete masterpiece of God's picture of marriage. That is a fact.

Once I realized this, I was blown away. Since this is a secret mystery, how then can I seek God to find it out? Remember, I still need to find out myself so I can please my future wife!

As I searched the Bible, I came across many scriptures showing that God does reveal secrets and mysteries. All these scriptures say so:

- "He revealeth the deep and secret things: he knoweth what is in the darkness, and the light dwelleth with him" (Daniel 2:22).
- "Then was the secret revealed unto Daniel in a night vision. Then Daniel blessed the God of heaven" (Daniel 2:19).
- "But as for me, this secret is not revealed to me for any wisdom that I have more than any living, but for their sakes" (Daniel 2:30).

- "For there is nothing hidden, which shall not be manifested; neither was any thing kept secret, but that it should come abroad" (Mark 4:22).
- "It is the glory of God to conceal a thing: but the honour of kings is to search out a matter" (Proverbs 25:2).
- "The secret things belong unto the Lord our God: but those things which are revealed belong unto us and to our children forever" (Deuteronomy 29:29).
- "The secret of the Lord is with them that fear him; and he will shew them his covenant" (Psalm 25:14).

These scriptures confirmed for me that God does in fact reveal secrets. I was on the hunt, and I was getting closer! In 1 Corinthians 13:2, the writer Paul mentions, "he was given the gift of prophecy, and could understand all mysteries...." After reading this scripture repeatedly, coupled with my new understanding that God reveals secrets, my mind was illuminated. The words *understand all mysteries* leaped off the page. At that moment, I felt like God was telling me Paul was able to understand all mysteries, which meant so could I! Including the mystery of marriage! And if I can understand, you most certainly can too. You see, Romans 2:11 says that "there is no respect of persons with God." This means what He has done for one, He will do for another. All we have to do is ask!

I went back to my original scripture in Ephesians 5:31–32, and I kept on reading: "For this cause shall a man leave his father and mother, and be joined unto his wife, and they two shall be one flesh. This is a great mystery." In the next verse, Paul touches on the key to understanding this mystery when he says, "But I speak concerning Christ" (this is the key), and he includes something else: "And the Church." And then in verse 33, he says, "Nevertheless." In modern-day terms, this could be interpreted as meaning "But anyway" or "But I won't get into that right now." So he concludes his instruction about marriage and says, "Let every one of you in particular so love his wife even as himself; and the wife see that she reverence her husband."

Let me explain what just happened in those few verses. The writer, Paul, "who understands all mysteries," was writing about marriage. He takes us, the reader, back to what God said to Adam and Eve in the beginning, and then he tells us how marriage is a mystery. Then he touches on the mystery aspect, saying, "I'm speaking right now about Christ and his Church." However, this is very brief because if Paul were to take the time to explain this entire mystery to them, it would be enough to write a whole separate book solely on that subject. At the present time, he was only writing a letter to give some simple instructions. So he touches on the secret to the mystery and then gets back to his instructions for husbands to love their wives and wives to honor their husbands. But for those who want more, he leaves a subtle bread crumb that will lead us to what it would take to understand the mystery of marriage.

If you are still confused about the key, then let me state it plainly. Paul is saying if you want to understand the mystery of marriage between a man and woman, then you must understand the relationship between Christ and his Church. Christ in the scriptures depicts a husband. The Church (which is the single term in the Bible that embodies all the people of God) depicts a bride. Christ is the *true* husband, and his people are the *true* bride. The traditional physical ceremony we all have come to know at a wedding or marriage is only a tangible (visible) depiction of the spiritual (invisible) coming together in a relationship between Christ and his born-again people.

If you do not know Christ and have a revelation of this relationship, then your marriage will never reach its full potential. A husband's relationship with his wife is designed by God to mirror Christ's passionate love for his people (the Church, his bride).

You cannot understand this relationship until you first come to know Christ in your own personal relationship. Once you have a relationship with Christ, like any other relationship, he will begin to communicate with you and reveal things to you. If someone has a secret, the only way to get it is to go to the person and ask them to share it with you. Or you have to go to someone else who knows that person and ask them to tell you what it is. For those who know Christ, what's written in this book is only the tip of the iceberg. You can begin to ask him to reveal more. For those who have not yet met Christ, you will have the opportunity to invite Him into your heart by reading the short prayer at the back of this book.

Now let us take a journey into the mind of God and see if we can get a glimpse of this relationship. Let us use the master key and study Christ.

# CHAPTER 3

# Touched by Her Infirmities

Have you ever had a manager or supervisor who you felt was inconsiderate, unfair, and challenging to work with? On the other hand, have you experienced having a manager or supervisor who was compassionate, thoughtful, and considerate of others? They were awesome, and it was a pleasure working for them. In many cases, you will find that the inconsiderate boss didn't work their way up into their management role but rather were brought in to replace someone else. In these situations, the manager lacks the relevant insights of your job, function, and role and therefore fails to understand your work. They lack compassion because they have not felt personally what it takes to fulfill your position and do it well!

The compassionate supervisor is much different. Often it's because this person has shared or similar work experience. They have been where you are and experienced what you are experiencing, and they have *felt* it personally. That's what makes them so understanding. They have felt your pain and empathize with you from having felt what you are feeling. Many times, this person makes an awesome boss.

Christ told me, "This principle is what's going to make you a better husband." The Bible says in Hebrews 4:15, "For we have not a high priest [Jesus] which cannot be touched with the feelings of our infirmities [weaknesses, problems, cares, and concerns], but was in all points tempted as we yet are." What this is saying is that Jesus Christ (the true husband), our advocate, is qualified to be such a great advocate and intercessor on our behalf because he came down and became human. He, being human, experienced in every manner and in every way what we experience. He understands what it feels like to be hungry, thirsty, afraid, tired, angry, annoyed, tempted, sad, happy, in pain, heartbroken, betrayed, talked about, hated, unappreciated, misunderstood, taken advantage of, liked, disliked, sincerely loved, loved for wrong motives—the whole nine yards. One could say He has been in our "position" and was quite successful at it!

Therefore, he is touched (or can empathize) with our feelings, our emotions, and our weaknesses. He is able to show grace, have compassion, be patient, and bear with us in all things because he knows exactly how we feel and what we are going through. He was once there. Christ (the true husband) is a great lover to his people (his bride) because He was once where they were. Christ told me that, because I belong to him, spiritually I *am his bride*, and I must love my wife like He loves me. You know what it feels like to be a wife and to be in her position. You know how it feels to submit to me even when I haven't given you the entire picture with all the details. You know what it feels like to not understand and, despite all your emotions, to still have to trust me. You know what it feels like to make a mistake and not want me to scorn you, get upset, or say I told you so.

He said, "Treat her like I treat you. When you make a mistake, in most cases, you already know you screwed up. You are already sad and upset with yourself, and your emotions are frantic because of the situation you have caused. When you come to me, as your loving husband, I will love on you and support you in fixing the problem. I have patience with you *and* all your emotions. Love her like I love you. You will be able to do this because you, too, will be touched by the feelings of her infirmities, emotions and all. Remember, you were and are the same way."

Now you see why you *must* be in a relationship with Christ in order to do this. We will touch further on this throughout the entire book.

# CHAPTER 4

# Cherish Her–She Is Precious

"Where purpose is unknown, abuse is inevitable." This is a simple statement, but it's profound. Whenever you don't know the reason why something exists, it's very hard to appreciate its value. Let's take something simple for example, like our eyelashes. Do we really pay much attention to how important they are? Some tend to think they're only useful when wearing mascara; however, that is not their purpose. Having beautiful, full eyelashes is great, but your eyelashes are there as a first line of defense for your eyes, keeping airborne dirt, dust, lint, and other debris from reaching the delicate eye tissues. When the eyes are open, eyelashes catch some airborne debris, but when the eyes are closed, they form a nearly impenetrable barrier against foreign irritants. It's something so simple but extremely important!

*Just like every other thing that God created, the woman was also formed with purpose. If you do not know her purpose, you will not place the proper value on her.*

The Bible says that the sons of God (angels) came down from heaven and saw how glorious the women of Earth were. It goes on to say that the woman was so fair that the angels of God broke God's law, took for themselves women from the earth to mate with, thus creating a breed of giants (Gen. 6:2–4). This is intriguing because you have to remember that these "sons of God" came from heaven itself, where the streets are gold and everything created is perfect. What could be more glorious than that? I would submit to you that these angels from heaven were so blown away by the existence and beauty of women because even though heaven was amazing, women did not exist there. They were so floored by women because a woman had never been seen before! They did not exist until there was a need and purpose for them. Since man was not created in heaven but on Earth, there wasn't any creature called "woman" ever in heaven. One of the purposes of males and females was to reproduce. In heaven, the angels don't reproduce; they are created. The woman was not created there. God created her from man on Earth. She was made because man did not have a mate that was meet, or "suitable," for him.

*You should cherish the woman because God specifically tailor-made her to meet your need.* She was brought into existence only on planet Earth where man was as the answer to what man was looking for. She is God's answer for a man.

Jesus later speaks about what heaven will be like in the future and specifically says there is no marriage there, and people are not given in marriage. There is no gender; we are all spirits at that time (Matt. 22:28–30). In the beginning, God made the man, Adam, gave him a mission to do on the earth, and formed a woman who was specifically tailored to help him complete the mission God gave him. This is a universal principle for every man and his wife. Once a man finds God and discovers his purpose and mission on Earth, *his* wife should be meet, suitable, or unique to help complete the God-given eternal and divine task that God has specifically given *them*.

Every couple does not have the same mission. Another man's wife will not be "suitable" or possess the same gifts, qualities, talents that she would need to help with that unique mission. If God is calling me to be a sailor, then my wife should probably not be afraid of water, and it would be good if she knew how to swim. You need to cherish *your* wife and realize that there are certain qualities she has that no other woman will possess. No two people are the same. You will not find another just like her. How valuable is something that is one of a kind in the world? I read in a magazine about a foreign car company that made a limited edition car; only seven of them exist in the world. The value of those cars ranged in the multimillions because of their rarity. When you realize your wife is a "limited edition," the only one made in the world, you will see her true value and begin to cherish her as such.

# CHAPTER 5

# The Test of Faithfulness

The Bible asks how a man can say he loves God, whom he cannot see, and hate his brother, whom he can see. This principle raises the question: If you can't love your visible neighbor, then how will you love God, who is invisible? However, concerning my wife or mate, the Lord told me to use this principle in reverse. The Lord had me realize that, as a single person, I must realize that my first lesson in marriage and faithfulness was to understand that I am spiritually his bride as a member of the body of Christ. That means once I became saved, I essentially entered into a marriage covenant and am now married to him. Hence, the scripture refers to his people as "the bride of Christ." I am his bride, and he is my husband (spiritually speaking).

He said I must first learn to be faithful to him. Spiritually married, I would learn that despite all the other attractive options the world would present me, I would learn not to cheat on, fornicate, or commit adultery on him. He showed me that as long as I was in this world, attractive things would come my way. The world would walk past me with the charms of riches, fame, wisdom, prominence, knowledge, power—all the attractive and desirable temptations of the human heart. If I could successfully remain faithful, loyal, and devoted to him (God), whom I can't physically see, then practicing this would build the discipline needed for faithfulness. When proven faithfulness is shown, we are then ready for a physical marriage.

I would have no problem remaining faithful to my wife, who would be right in front of my face, if I could discipline myself to remain faithful to my unseen God. As a married man, no matter what other female might cross my path, despite how tempting or attractive she may be, I would have already learned what it meant to remain faithful to the one I was in covenant with. The Lord told me, "If you could not remain faithful to me, how do you expect to do it with your wife?" Many men never learn this lesson, and that is why they are struggling to find the power within themselves to resist temptation and not cheat. God does not want you to learn this *after* you get married. There are mistakes in learning. You should understand this *before* you walk into a marriage.

# CHAPTER 6

# Submission: Partially or Fully—You Choose!

How can I ensure my wife will be submissive to me? The Lord told me, "Tyler, remember, even though you may be single, you currently remain married to me. You are my bride, and I am your husband." He said, "Remember my Word. I told you, 'Be not deceived. God is not mocked, for whatsoever a man soweth, that shall he also reap'" (Galatians 6:7).

God told me that you cannot sow "partial submission" (to him) and reap "full submission" from her. He said, "If you look at someone's marriage and see that the wife is not completely submissive to her husband, that only means there is some area in my Word in which he is not completely submitted to me. He's only reaping what he's sowing." God told me, "Son, if you want your wife to submit to you, then you must completely be submissive to me and my Word."

Wow! How many men don't realize this and are struggling trying to get their wives to submit in their marriage, not realizing there is a prerequisite for this? You must qualify for submission. Your complete submission to the Lord is required. Submission is a beautiful thing. It is designed to remove burdens and relieve stress. To trust that someone has your best interest in mind is a blessing. Submission is an act of the will and cannot be forced but given willingly. When applied correctly, it is a very powerful and beautiful thing.

# Seven Spokes That Make Her Wheel Turn

There are seven areas in which a woman needs to have complete assurance and satisfaction to make the marriage wheel roll. Every area must be in place, and not one can be ignored. Your wife must be taken care of

- mentally
- emotionally
- physically
- financially
- spiritually
- intellectually
- sexually

The Bible says we are to love (take care of) our wife in the same way that Christ takes care of the Church. He does this in every way. We can look at these seven areas and how Christ ministers to his bride (the Church) in each area.

## Mentally

We will look at the mind as spoke one. The Bible says in Ephesians 5:23, "For the husband is the head of the wife, even as Christ is the head of the church." Most people read this and go directly to the head meaning authority, or the one who calls the shots, but the head is really referring to the order of God. It is a position of responsibility. Let's take an even closer look at this word head. What lies within the head? Of course, the mind or brain, right? This in no way means the husband is the only brain in the relation, but rather as husband and wife you should be thinking on one accord with each other in unity. Obviously, both individuals have a part in this. Each person has to communicate, but for now, I want to address specifically the role of the husband in helping to shape his wife's mind—more specifically her thinking. Romans 12:2 tells us not to be conformed to the world's way of thinking but to have our minds renewed. No one in the relationship is impervious to wrong thinking or sometimes getting off. We all have our own battles with our thoughts and there can be external influences that impact our thinking. The devil knows how powerful it is for a husband and wife to agree and be unified for a righteous purpose. Therefore, he tirelessly works to get both parties to either disagree, causing conflict, or to agree together to sin. If he can get one person's thinking off, he knows the other will be more easily swayed and likely to follow.

Remember when God told Abraham he and Sarah would have a child? The angels came to visit Abraham to tell him this, the bible says when his wife heard, she laughed. Then the angel asked Abraham why she laughed? Because Abraham wasn't assisting in shaping Sarah's thinking in this one area the devil was able to sneak in and plant in Sarah the contrary idea of having her husband sleep with another woman. Abraham, although knowing what God said and promised, eventually capitulated to the sin. This flesh idea brought forth Ishmael, whom the world is still having to deal with today. We can clearly see how wrong thinking can lead a relationship or family down a path of destruction. Let me also mention that in this example, Sarah was the one who happened to introduce the idea; however, I can think of twice as many examples in the bible where kings, priests, husbands, (in other words, the men) got off and completely had wrong thinking.

We must understand that we as husbands may not be right all the time and know when to humble ourselves and have our own thinking realigned. We can't be so prideful to not know when to listen to our wives. Husbands, let's do our part to listen, communicate and as much as possible take the responsibility of ensuring that you and your wife are not only thinking together on one accord but on the right accord.

## Emotionally

For the second spoke, let's address the emotions. Husbands, you must not fail in this area of ministry to your wife. Realize that your wife is an emotional being. You should now have an understanding of this, realizing how you act yourself when it comes to the Lord. Whatever emotions you are having, the Lord *does not* say, "Suck it up" and just ignore them. He tends to every emotion you have. If you are fearful, He tends to the fear. If you are saddened, He tends to your sadness. If you are angry, He deals with your anger. If you are worried or have anxiety, He brings reassurance. If you are joyful, he is joyful along with you. When you get excited about something, he is excited too! There is not an emotion that you have that the Lord is not right there with you. We tend to only focus on being there for the negative times, but God not only holds you to comfort you in sorrow. He is also there to raise his hand with yours and give you a high five when you get excited about something. Husbands, it is very important that you meet this need. Because women are emotional beings, they can't function properly without these needs being met. If you are not meeting them, they will seek them elsewhere for sheer survival. Let's just hope she seeks it from the Lord. You don't want her to seek it from another man.

## Physically

The third spoke is physically. It's our job to physically take care of our wives. The Bible speaks of "dressing and keeping" as you would tend to a garden. In the same way, Christ says that He is coming for the Church, "a wife" that is without spot, wrinkle, or blemish, a dazzling Church arrayed in fine clothing, decked out in sparkling jewelry of all precious stones, clothed in honor and glory and lavished with all desirable gifts. And for what reason? That He might present her to himself.

Your wife shouldn't always look tired, beaten, used up, and trodden down. If she does, then you are not being a great husband. The Bible says she is a reflection of you. Man is made in the reflection and image and glory of God, and the woman is the glory of the man (1 Corinthians 11:7). Since Christ makes sure his bride is decked out because she is a reflection of him, we as husbands ought to do the same.

So what does this look like? Before we get to shower them with gifts, let's start with the basics. It looks like this. When you see her trying to lift something too heavy for her back, you go run and lift it for her. She should never have to lift, hold, or carry anything that causes her to strain. That's wear and tear on her body that was never designed to handle such heavy weight like that. Your body was made to handle that, not hers. If you sit there and watch your wife strain her arms, her back, or any other muscle on her body, then you are "abusing" her. Her body's delicate and should be treated as such.

What else does that look like? It means if she has been standing up all day and her feet ache, you give her a foot massage. It means if her back does hurt, you give her a back rub. If her neck hurts, you tend to that, and if her shoulder hurts, you tend to that too. You want to always tend to the condition of your wife's body because you want her to look good and feel good for as long as she's on Earth.

This also includes the upkeep of her hair, nails, make-up—everything on her body requires maintenance.

As that is being continued, you want to make sure she has funds to now dress her well-kept body. She needs money to shop for clothes to put on. Depending on your budget, you can work that out. But there is no need for having a well-kept body and not having beautiful attire to put on it. This is important. Your wife needs to be able to have nice attire.

Next, we move on to the jewelry. Earrings, necklaces, rings, and bracelets all add to her dazzling appearance. You want to lavish her with all kinds of different gifts to keep her looking nice and make her feel valuable and, most of all, just show her how much you love her. The Bible says, "For God so loved…that he *gave*." A part of showing her you love her is giving gifts. Some men try to only do the gift part while ignoring everything else. *This will not work.*

## Financially

Imagine if, once we got saved, God told us, "I will never leave or forsake you. I will always be with you. When times get tough, you can always talk to me, whether you are happy, sad, angry, agitated, tired, stressed, or confused, and I will always be there. However, as far as your needs and comforts on Earth are concerned, you are on your own! I can't help you with that part."

You would probably tell him, "well, God, if you gave me some money, I probably wouldn't have to come to you with half of those things!"

If God truly loves us, you would think he wouldn't leave us to fend for ourselves in a world where money is the currency whereby all our needs are met. This is why Philippians 4:19 states, "But my God shall supply all your need according to his riches in glory by Christ Jesus."

Another scripture states, "Now unto him that is *able* to do exceedingly abundantly above all that we ask or think [emphasis mine]." The financial spoke is important.

As the husband, you must ensure that your wife, your bride, is taken care of financially. This means she need not worry about keeping the lights on, the water running, the cable bills, a house over her head, and a nice bed to sleep in. She also needs her own money. God gives us our own money, and we have the freedom to manage it according to what's on our hearts to do. We have the freedom to spend it on ourselves or on other people we love, give some to the poor, or start a business, or we can even bless him by giving it back to him as a gift. He allows us to express who we are and do with it as we please. Once your wife isn't concerned with holding on to every dime she has out of fear of lacking a need, you can do what God does, which is give her riches freely to just enjoy!

I would also like to talk about the seriousness of what can happen when this is not done. It only takes one time for you to drop the ball on this for fear and doubt to creep into her heart. Fear of not completely trusting you to take care of financial needs will result in the law of self-preservation. She will begin to create backup plans. This can be manifested in hiding money and keeping secrets. Anything done in the dark will create distrust and division, which can ruin a marriage. This type of doubt and fear can also result in the temptation to find other means and sources of getting financial needs met. It can leave the door open for third parties. It may not be that she doesn't love you; it may be simply her trying to survive. Make sure you are a good provider. This will keep your marriage intact.

## Spiritually

This spoke is probably one of the most misunderstood and oftentimes left out completely as a need. The main reason is that many people don't understand the spiritual because it is unseen. However, though unseen, it is the *most important* spoke in this wheel. Every human being has a spiritual need. We are spirits, we possess souls, and we live in bodies.

The Word of God is the only thing that promotes spiritual growth. The Bible says this: "Husbands, love your wives, even as Christ loved the church [his bride/wife] and gave himself for it; That he might sanctify and cleanse it with the washing of water by the Word." This is even how it was done in the very first marriage ever with Adam and Eve. The bible says that after God planted Adam in the garden and gave him instructions to dress and keep it, he then gave him a commandment saying "Of every tree of the garden thou mayest freely eat: but of the tree of the knowledge of good and evil, thou shalt not eat of it:" Genesis 2:16-17. In the very next verse (Genesis 2:18) God then stakes that it is not good that man should be alone, and he would make for Adam help that was suitable for him. In my opinion this would lead me to believe that in this instance Eve had not been created yet, thus was not present to hear this commandment. Later on in this chapter it goes on to talk about how God walked in the garden with both Adam and Eve; clearly displaying how he speaks to both the husband and with together. However, what God spoke to Adam alone I believe he was expected to share that with his wife. We know Adam in fact did share what God commanded him, because when being tempted by the serpent Eve quoted God's exact commandment even though she initially wasn't there when it was spoken. I believe because God spoke to Adam first directly, God held him accountable. Even though eve had already eaten from the forbidden tree, the judgment did not come until after she gave it to her husband and Adam ate.

In many relationships today, it seems like the role has been reversed. Many women realize first the need for spiritual growth and, in turn, end up trying to drag their husbands to church. This should not be so. Husbands, you and your wife's spiritual health are *mandatory* for the healthy existence of your marriage. The Bible says, "The spirit of a man will sustain his infirmity, but who can survive a wounded spirit?" What is this proverb saying? It's saying that even if you get physically weak or tired and stressed out, and you feel like needs are not being met how you would like, and at the time you would like, and your feet hurt, and your back is sore, and money isn't there, and you're being tempted…that if your spirit is strong and healthy, it will sustain you through it all.

Many relations and marriages fall apart because, under the stress of trying to roll year after year on broken spokes because the spiritual spoke was never in place, people are not strong enough to keep going. The wheel stops.

The scripture talks about the washing of water by the Word. Picture a small basin large enough to fit just your feet in. Imagine that little basin has water in it, and it's half full. Now imagine that water signifies how much of the Word of God you know. Now imagine how hard it would be to wash a full-grown person with that little bit of water. Many husbands are walking around with a cup full of Word. There is no way you can wash or cleanse and sanctify (which means "set apart") your wife with that little bit of Word. In fact, what's happening is the opposite. Women are in the churches getting the Word and then trying to tell the husbands what "sayest the Lord." The only problem with that is this. The Bible says the husband is the head. What this means is this: God will speak directly to the husband for the specific mission and vision God has for him and his family. The husband, as head, is then supposed to communicate the mission and instructions God has given him to his wife and then to the children.

Your wife is set apart because each family has a different mission. Your wife is created to help you with the specific mission he has given you and your family. You all need to know the written Word of God, but the Word God has spoken to the man must be given to the wife. This sanctifies her and sets her apart for the specific and unique mandate that she has as the helper to support the husband in bringing about the vision God has given them. This is not a game. We are talking about completing God-given mandates. And husbands, you need your wives' help.

If you didn't, He would not have given you one. This is serious business. Read the Bible. Go to church. Seek the instructions for your family. Tell your wife what the plan is. Let her help you. That is what God created her for.

## Intellectually

This particular spoke is another one that is seldom talked about. Remember, you are to love your wife as Christ loves you. He is full of wisdom and knowledge. He knows everything about everything. So how does this come into play regarding your relationship with your wife?

I will tell you. Jesus Christ isn't boring! Nor is He dumb. Because He created everything in the universe, He can enlighten us about so much. One of the keys to having a fresh and exuberant relationship is learning and being exposed to new things.

Christ himself is the most interesting being that ever has existed. He is also the most intelligent being that ever has existed. Our relationship with him is not stale, monotonous, boring, or predictable. As we continue in our relationship with him, He continually blows our minds by showing us things we don't know, taking us places we've never been, and teaching us what we don't know. When we have a question, He has an answer.

God is always exposing us to something that stimulates our minds. Keeping our interest and attention.

Leaving us wanting more. This aids in keeping the relationship fresh. As we continue to grow and evolve, we should have the mindset that there is always something new we can learn and discover.

I'm not saying that we have to be like Christ and know every answer to every question our wives ask. We cannot do that. That is impossible. What I'm saying is this. You can pick up a book, read some magazines, find out what her interests are, and learn more about that subject. Learn about some subjects that don't even interest her at all. You want to be able to tell her something she doesn't know about. Have something new and interesting come out of your mouth that she hasn't heard before, something enlightening, something new, something that will stimulate her mind. Make her think. Make her ponder. Broaden her insight. You want to try and take her somewhere she hasn't been. Let her behold something with her eyes—new scenery, a mountain range, a valley, a painting, and so on. You both will grow closer as you experience things together. The relationship never grows stale but remains new and fresh.

Make yourself interesting. You also want to be interesting yourself. One thing that is so awesome about our relationship with Christ is that we don't have to go off to the Grand Canyon for him to show us something new. There are times when we just sit at home alone and He begins to reveal more about himself! When you love someone, you want to get to know more about that person and everything about that person. In the same way we spend time alone with Christ getting to know his multifaceted person and allowing him to open up and reveal the things on his heart and mind, As husband and wife we should be mirroring the same effort of affinity towards one another. This is a whole other level of intimacy that has nothing to do with having intercourse. It has to do with really getting to know a person on a deeper inner level, a heart level. Having the privilege to know your innermost thoughts is a right that is supposed to be sacred to your wife; it's hers and hers only. After opening up to her on this level emotionally and spiritually and allowing her to have access to your very soul (which is the invisible *real* part of you), you will find that your feelings and passion for each other grow so deep, strong, forceful, and intense that they will then naturally compel you both to want to express what you are feeling on the inside. Sex or intercourse is the physical expression of the inner passion you have for each other.

The longer you are in the relationship, the more you find out about each other. The more you find out about each other, the closer you get to each other. The closer you get to each other, the more oneness you share. The deeper and more intense your passion becomes, the more compelled you are to express it, which results in greater and deeper and more intense sex. This brings me to the seventh spoke: satisfying her sexually.

## Sexually

*Sex versus Making Love*

Sex is intimacy. When many people think of sex, they do not think of God. Most people get silent in a church or would never mention God and sex in the same sentence. They think sex is some unholy activity to be ashamed of when, in fact, it is the exact opposite. God is a loving, deeply passionate, and extremely intimate God. He loves intimacy. He wants to be "in" us and wants us "in" him to the point that we become one with him.

When a man, a husband, becomes intimate with his wife, she surrenders her entire self and willingly lets him come into her, and they experience a closeness and a oneness. You actually become one spirit and one body. When you are one with the Lord, you never have to speak or tell him anything. He knows you, and He knows your thoughts. He knows what you want, when you want it, and how you want. So it is with husband and wife. When both of you are one with the Spirit of God and become one with each other, you are then literally joined together. He feeds you her thoughts, feelings, needs, desires, and pleasures. When being intimate with each other, you will intuitively know exactly what to do, what to say, where she wants to be rubbed, where she wants you to touch her, how to caress her, when to grab her, how fast, how slow, when to kiss, where to kiss, how to kiss, when and where to lick, when and where and how and what body part to suck, which leg to lift, how high to lift it, and so on. Of course, this will be unique to whatever your partner likes and needs for that particular night.

The marriage covenant mimics the relationship that an individual has with Jesus. Jesus knows what mood you are in, and He will minister to your need for how you are feeling at that moment or that day or that night. We don't always want and need the same thing over and over. Our desires change, and so does your wife's. You must be Spirit-led to get in tune to fulfill her desire and meet her pleasure needs for that night. God's way is so that you might experience sex and experience it more fully. He will tell you exactly what she wants, as he himself lives within her. As God is the center of the relationship, the same three-cord principle of the Holy Trinity (God the Father, God the Son, God the Holy Spirit) will be at work—three entities yet connected with one Spirit. Have fun with this spoke.

# CHAPTER 8

# The Filter of Love

You have heard the saying "beauty is in the eye of the beholder." That simply means the appreciation of an object being viewed does not depend necessarily on the object itself, but rather on the person viewing the object. A person can also see a thing differently depending on the type of lens they are looking through. You ever look at a couple and asked yourself the question "what does he/she see in them?" It doesn't matter whether you can see it or not. They are in love and probably see each other through a lens that has been filtered through love. Love tends to act as a filter, leaving the purest form of a substance. It's how God views us, and it's how we should view our wives.

Every woman wants to feel and look beautiful. God has designed the woman with certain features that naturally attract a man to her. A husband should desire his wife, and your wife needs to know that you think she is beautiful. She needs to know that you desire her. She needs to hear, see, and feel your genuine desire for her beauty, inside and out. You express your feelings toward her not only with your words but also with your actions.

Sadly, in today's world, society tends to project images of what it thinks beauty is. Beauty in the world has been influenced by media outlets, movies, supermodels, the rich and famous, and many photoshopped pictures. The media has dictated to many what the world's concept of beauty is, which in my opinion is inaccurate because beauty is subjective. This could cause problems in people's relationships because your mate may not look like the image of beauty that the media portrays.

God explained to me how He sees me. He says I am beautiful and fearfully and wonderfully made. He shows me how He sees me through the eyes of love or through the filter of love. Remember, a filter is designed to sift through everything that is not good and only keep the good.

As you look at your wife through the eyes of love, she does not have any flaws. All you see is perfection. Beauty no longer is what the world says but is defined now by whatever your wife looks like. Your definition of beauty is now her. Many women are concerned and often worried about always looking beautiful. Consumed by the pressure to wake up beautiful, go to bed beautiful, and remain beautiful in between.

They are even more concerned about how they look when pregnant or if they gain a little weight. But this does not matter in your eyes. However she looks at the time represents what beauty is to you. This can only happen through the love of God.

You cannot obtain these "glasses" naturally, but they are spiritual glasses that God puts on your eyes. When you look into her eyes and tell her how beautiful she is, you aren't lying. You are wholeheartedly telling the absolute truth with all sincerity, with all conviction, and with all passion. You truly see her beauty, and you only have eyes for her. You only desire her because, in your eyes, she is what beauty looks like. As you look at her, speak to her, and express to her how beautiful she is, she will see the sincerity in your eyes. She will hear the passion in your voice. She will have no doubt in her mind that what you say is true. She will walk around feeling confident and with assurance, knowing her husband thinks she is beautiful. It's like adding water and sunlight to a flower.

# CHAPTER 9

# Unconditional Love: God's Ideal Relationship

We are to love our wives as Christ loves the Church, and the way that Christ loves his Church is unconditional. *Unconditional* means that there are no conditions under which he will stop loving us. In some relationships, there are conditions on love. If they treat me right, I love them. If they do what I say, I love them. If they never cheat, I love them. The only problem with this thinking is that whatever *that* is, it is the condition under which you are saying your love will cease. Remember, God's love has no conditions, so there is nothing we could do or say that would make him stop loving us. He only has one mode. A light switch has on and off. God only has on. If you were to turn a light on, the rays of light do not care what they are shining on. It could be a penny. It could be a bird. It could be an angry dog. The light doesn't care.

God's unconditional love is not based on emotions because that would make it based on his choice. Once you choose that you will love her no matter what and make that decision, there will be no conditions under which you stop. This is God's love, and this is how He commands us to love our wives.

CHAPTER 10

# The Enlargement of the Heart: Pour Out Your Love

Ephesians 3:19 talks about knowing the love of God, which passes all understanding. It mentions knowing the breadth, the height, the width, and the depth of love. The Bible says that the love of God is shed abroad in our hearts. Another translation says that the love of God is poured into our hearts by the Holy Spirit. When I read that phrase, "poured into our hearts," I envision a gallon tub being poured into a cup. If God is a gallon tub, your heart will be the cup, and his love is poured inside.

Before we loved our wives, we dated (or courted) them. So let's take a moment to talk about dating. David was the wisest king, and his son was the wisest human to every walk this Earth. If you study them, you will see that King Solomon asked God for wisdom, and the Bible says that God enlarged his heart.

What this means is that by enlarging Solomon's heart, God increased his capacity to understand. For example, if most people can contain a cup full of wisdom, God spiritually enlarged Solomon's heart whereby he could contain not just a cupful, but an ocean full of the wisdom of God. Proof of Solomon's increased capacity was in his ability to operate in wisdom and physically manifest the spiritual wisdom that was inside of him.

Solomon built houses, orchards, gardens, an irrigation system—you get the idea. He was brilliant. He had horses and chariots, fortified cities, and weapons of warfare beyond what had been seen during that time. Solomon was able to manifest God's supernatural wisdom in a manner that could be seen and experienced, so much so that people from afar would travel to see it for themselves.

Solomon was not the only instance in the bible where God increased someone's capacity for more. In Psalms, it talks about the enlargement of the heart. David (Solomon's father) asked God to enlarge his heart to increase his capacity to love. Again, this means asking for your capacity to contain to be enlarged so that more can be poured into you. God is love, and if you want to love anyone, in particular your spouse or your wife, you must know God. The more you know God, the more you can comprehend. The more you understand God, who is love, the more you will be able to clearly articulate and pour out his love into someone else.

As I began to understand the concept of increased capacity, I prayed and asked the Lord to enlarge my heart. I wanted to comprehend the greatest depth of love. And what did God do? He began to expand my heart! He began to pour out his love on me. The best way I can describe what happened is that it was like I was standing in a beautiful paradise under a rushing waterfall, and that waterfall was pouring down on me. I was being drowned in this waterfall of God's love!

Have you ever turned a faucet on? Not just a little bit either, but all the way until the knob can no longer turn? This is the fastest and the hardest that the faucet can pour out the water. As I stood under the waterfall, it was like God was controlling the flow much like a faucet. Just when I thought the waterfall had been turned on all the way, it was as if God created a new knob and turned it on harder. And then He kept turning harder and harder. His love was being poured on me to the point where I couldn't take it anymore. It was overwhelming.

As I felt the love of God being poured out on me to the point where it was unbearable, I simultaneously didn't want it to stop because it began to feel good. How could I want something to stop and yet keep going at the same time? God had to explain to me that to love your wife like Christ loved the Church, you need to pour out your love on her in the same manner. The only way to do this is to enlarge your heart so much that your capacity to contain is that of an ocean. With a greater capacity, the more you can pour on her. Your container should be so large that you literally pour out your love on her to the point where she doesn't understand it, it's incomprehensible, and she can no longer bear it. That is your goal: to pour out your love on her until she is running over,, drenched and cannot bear the force of the magnitude of the rushing water of your love.

# CHAPTER 11

# Driven by Perfect (Mature) Love

Marriage is God-ordained and God-approved for his creation. In my opinion, there would be many more marriages today if men weren't so reluctant of marriage out of fear of failure. Failure to adequately provide for his wife and for his household. Failure to make his wife happy. Failure to be a good husband. Failure to hold it together. The weight and pressure of being responsible for the well-being of the household ultimately are the husband's to carry. A lot of men actually do want to get married and love the women they are with; they are just unsure whether they can handle it all.

There is an answer to this very real and common problem. I, too, was thinking this, and I asked the Lord, "Lord, how can I ensure that I won't fail in the position as husband and head of my household? Life can be tough, God. How can I ensure the well-being of my wife and children in a world that seems like it offers no mercy?"

Here was his answer: the Lord assured me that, just like the Church, his bride does not have to handle everything on their own. And when they don't know what to do, they seek Christ, whom the Bible calls the husband, for answers. So it will be for you. He told me that my wife and children look to me as the head, so I then in turn should look to him for what to do. Remember, God is love. The Bible says in 1 Corinthians 13:8 that charity (love) never fails. God is the only one who always has an answer, always knows what to do, always has a plan, always has a way, is always trustworthy, always reliable, always dependable, and simply cannot fail. Most men think they must carry this weight alone. Because we are human, we have limitations. We cannot predict the future, and we don't have all the answers. It is so important to know that as the head of the household, we can lean on and look to the one who does. The Lord has promised that He can and will meet every need. It pleased me to know that while I thought ultimately the responsibility weighed solely on me, it in fact really falls on God. He is the one who knows the future and sees all. As a husband and father and as head of the household, I am to get my direction from him! The Lord will always lead us to a good place.

This is his plan for guaranteed success for our families! Wouldn't you be more confident if you had a plan that could not fail? Rather than being afraid of marriage, we can walk in confidence and excitement about one of the most natural things that God intended for us to do on Earth, which is to start a family.

# CHAPTER 12

# Fidelity: The Test Drive (God. Your Invisible Partner)

One critical part of maintaining not only a blissful marriage but also a lasting one is remaining faithful to the person you love. There are many couples who begin with only having eyes for each other, but as time goes by, they experience an onslaught of distractions, temptations, and enticements that lure them away from their one true love. There can be a plethora of reasons this happens. Sometimes this is due to a deficit in an area in the relationship that is not being fulfilled, prompting a partner to seek fulfillment elsewhere. There are also cases in which some are drawn away unintentionally and unknowingly by outside forces that only appear to be more attractive and fulfilling than what they already have in front of them. Adultery is a huge problem in many of today's relationships. We must also keep in mind that cheating on a spouse is not limited to sexual acts only. There is also emotional adultery. Remaining faithful is crucial in sewing the tapestry of a beautiful marriage, and, being the creator, God, of course, knows this. His plan is for us to practice this faithfulness *first* with him.

When you begin your relationship with the Lord, He specifically says you are "spiritually" married to him. He warns us about not committing adultery on him with the world: "Ye adulterers and adulteresses, know ye not that the friendship of the world is enmity with God? Whosoever therefore will be a friend of the world is the enemy of God" (James 4:4).

Because God is a Spirit (John 4:24) and we cannot see him with our natural eyes or physically touch him, there is a strong inclination for us to be pulled away and enticed by things in the world that are extremely appealing to us. Many people are led away and enticed by the attractiveness of money, riches, fame, fortune, honor, and all the perks that come along with them. It is very easy to take your eyes off him to go spend time with and pursue something else that seems better and more fulfilling. When we are easily led away by things that seem attractive to us, God calls this committing adultery. What or who might you have you committed adultery against God with?

CHAPTER 13

# Make Her Blossom with Your Words

Have you ever heard of someone having a green thumb? This term is typically used for those who have the talent to plant, nurture, and grow anything green until it is exuberant, thriving, and flourishing, displaying the full, uniquely beautiful design it was created for. Many individuals who have green thumbs are considered valuable because there are many forms of plant life that seem to never grow and blossom to their full potential. They end up malnourished, and some wither away, never reaching their awe-inspiring beauty.

Much like what it would take for a plant or beautiful flower to blossom, we can take the same principle for what it takes to nourish your wife. I find it amazing that, much like a tree or a plant, the Bible says that "man" (humans) are made from the dust of the earth. What do plants and flowers need to grow?

Water and sunlight! One of the ways we water our wives is with our words (Eph. 5:26). We have heard of physical and verbal abuse; not speaking correctly to your wife, about your wife, or not speaking up for her will cause her leaves to wither. This type of talk does not help your wife grow into everything she is. It doesn't help her shine and exude her brilliant radiance from the inside out. It does the exact opposite.

Your words are extremely important. Criticizing instead of complementing, talking *at* instead of talking *to*, and tearing her down instead of building her up can stunt her growth. Criticizing her body parts, not speaking to her as an equal, never complimenting her, or not encouraging her in her uniqueness can tear down her self-esteem, leaving her feeling unappreciated and self-conscious. Once again, just like a plant needs water and sunlight to grow, your wife *needs* these things to grow and look and feel her best. Remember, watering a flower is not just a good thing to do; it is a necessity! A flower absolutely cannot grow without it.

Complimenting your wife is like pouring fresh water on her. You will even notice how she will literally brighten up, smile, and beam from ear to ear after receiving your words. This is like nourishment. Compliments shouldn't be limited to only her physical beauty. She is more than a face and a body. You should compliment all that she does—her cooking, her intellect, her creativity, things she may do around the house, her mothering skills, and all aspects that make up the unique individual who is now your wife. She will feel confident, appreciated, and valued on the inside. This inner feeling will seep out from the inside, resulting in a brighter smile and exuberant disposition.

It is also your duty to encourage your wife. The Bible mentions that we should love our wives as our own flesh and that no man has ever hated his own body. Knowing that you and your wife are one body, encouraging her not only benefits her, but it also lifts your entire body as a whole. Encouraging her is like encouraging yourself. As her life partner, you should be the person she can always turn to and expect positive reinforcement and assurance. Much like the brutal beating and erosion that plants endure from being exposed to the elements, your wife inevitably deals with outside storms, too, in the form of friendships, work, social pressures, and other common life occurrences.

Listening is a form of watering and nurturing. Any plant enthusiast will tell you that if you listen hard enough, the plant will tell you exactly what it needs. It may bend and lean toward the window. What is it saying? "I need more sunlight." The leaves may look brittle and brownish and begin to curl. It's saying, "I'm too dry; please water me." The leaves may look singed or blistered. It's saying, "I'm getting too much sunlight, and I'm burning." Your wife needs you to listen to what she has to say, both verbally and nonverbally. This is nourishing. It helps you to know what she needs more of and less of. You can tend to areas that need attention. Weather conditions can change, and plants need to be tended to accordingly in order to fully blossom. If you are not talking and listening to her, how will you know what conditions around her have changed? Listen attentively, and she will tell you what she needs.

# CHAPTER 14

# Become One

"For this cause shall a man leave his father and mother, and shall be joined unto his wife, and they two shall be one flesh" (Ephesians 5:13). There is much confusion about this particular scripture. How can two people join to become one? Of course, we know this is not saying that physically you and your wife become joined at the hip, but rather you begin to work together as one entity. There should be a clear goal or vision in the relationship that both man and woman are working together in unison to achieve. Many times, two people think that by coming together, they make each other complete. That is actually not the case. Two incomplete people do not make each other whole.

Look at it this way. Picture two whole pizza doughs on a counter. Each whole pizza covers two different areas on the counter. Once you roll the two whole pizza doughs together, they become one humongous pizza. The one whole pizza now has one purpose and covers more surface area on the countertop. In other words, two whole people coming together as one person now have a greater territory that they cover, and twice as much can be accomplished.

There also enters the capacity of a deeper level of intimacy that takes place when being joined together. This comes in the form of a unique spiritual bond that takes place during the union between a man and a woman. You can get to a place where you can be in tune with each other's thoughts, emotions, and wills (the soul).

## Becoming One

*Telepathy (Knowing without Her Saying)*
I have heard many men complain, saying how utterly ridiculous it is when their wife or girlfriend expects him to know what they want without having told him. "She thinks I'm a mind reader," they quip sarcastically, followed by "I don't read minds." This is what a lot of men complain about. Conversely, most women will tell you they don't want to have to tell their man "what they need." They continue, "Some things, if he really knew me and were in tune with me, I wouldn't have to say." This is the discussion going on during ladies' night.

Why is this feud universal with so many couples? While verbal communication is and will always be an integral pillar in every relationship, as a husband

and wife spiritually become one through sharing the same of God, there can be thoughts, feelings, and needs that need not be verbally expressed. God does not give us an intuitive desire that is not capable of being met. The Lord, in speaking about his Church, says things like "He knows what we have need of before we ask," "He can count the number of hairs on our head," and "He knows our thoughts from far off." Now, men, obviously, I'm not saying that we are like God and should be able to know everything about our spouses like him. But what I am saying is that these scriptures are our example of how detailed and how much attention He has for his Church. If we are given the commandment to love our wives like Christ loved the Church, then we are called to be in tune with them and give attention to their needs. The good thing is that God will help us with this. As we are Spirit-led, God, who should be at the center of the relationship between us and our wives, will speak to us regarding their needs. He can tell you things and point out details to help you fulfill what he has called you to do. You being intentional about being attentive, coupled with the Lord's help of being Spirit-led, can create a supernatural level of intimacy.

# CHAPTER 15

# Leading with Confidence

Luke 12:48 tells us, "To whom much is given, much is required." Anyone who has ever taken on any level of leadership can understand there comes a certain level of pressure and responsibility along with it. Becoming a husband is a great responsibility. Because of this, men can sometimes feel angst and hesitate before stepping into this role. Men have thoughts of doubt, insecurity, and inadequacy about whether they have what it takes to be successful. This is common when entering any role for the first time. What can help with this concern that many men go through is knowing that God has chosen them for this position.

God has chosen the man as the head of the family. He did not do this to make him a type of ruler or tyrant over the family, but because He is a God of order and not chaos. The Bible says God does everything decently and in order. You can also know that you are not alone in this leadership role. You have help. Understand that, yes, there is only one head on a body (naturally speaking), but on that head, there are two ears. That means that both you *and* your wife can hear from God to get direction. Notice also that on every head, there is only one mouth. Once you hear from God and discuss what direction to take, both of you should then be in agreement, of one accord, and speaking the same thing. A good leader recognizes great help.

## Christ Is Our Example

God has placed us in a position to lead. This is his will and his plan. Because it is his will and his plan, He also empowers and equips us to be leaders. One of the ways He does this is by being an example. Before anyone can become a good leader, they must first learn to follow. During our season of singleness and throughout life, we learn to follow God. We learn to go to him for answers to our questions, to get direction, to trust in him, and we learn by being recipients of how He leads and loves us. Christ is always looking and thinking ahead for things concerning the Church—his bride. Therefore, because He knows what is ahead, He already has made preparations concerning anything the Church may encounter. She doesn't have to concern herself over certain things because it is his job too.

He says in his Word to "take no thought concerning what we shall eat, how we shall dress." Will we have a place to live? How will we pay for it? Is my car working? These are questions of provision that a wife need not stress over. As a husband, you are called to always be thinking ahead about things concerning your wife, your children, and your household. When circumstances arrive, because you thought ahead, there should already be preparations made. She shouldn't have to worry because you are taking care of her. In essence, she should be able to cast her cares on you. You, in turn, can take those things to God.

Keep in mind that there will always be situations and circumstances that we cannot prepare for. We are not God and can't predict the future. We can, however, learn to go to God for what to do when unforeseen things happen. Remember, you have good help. The head has two ears. You and your wife can learn to go to God together to receive answers. You are a team. Good leaders know when to lead and when to listen. It doesn't matter which ear the words are spoken in because the entire head gets the answer. Trust that God has given you the ability to lead; go to him for answers, and use your help.

You are on a God-given mission, and she is helping you get there. It is part of her purpose! And she gets fulfillment from helping you.

The Bible says where there is no vision, the people perish. "Proverbs 29:18" In order to be a leader, you have to be leading people somewhere. You must have a clear vision of where you are going or what the mission is. Sometimes the details of exactly how to get there may come later or even as you go, but there must be a place you are going or a mission to accomplish. God does not create anything without a purpose. There is a purpose for you, there is a purpose for your wife, and there is a heavenly purpose to accomplish together. When God created Adam, He gave him work to do. This was a heavenly mandate. If you do not already know what God-given mandate He has for you to do here on Earth, then I would suggest you spend time in prayer to first find out what that is. It is hard to lead someone when you don't know where you are going. Ask God for the vision! Ask God what the mission is. Spend time in prayer to get this right. Help comes when there is a need for it. Remember that.

Use your help. Where purpose is unknown, abuse is inevitable. Understand and know that one of the deepest inner fulfillments your wife gets is when she is able to meet your needs. She will feel that way because when she is able to meet that need, she is actually fulfilling one of the purposes she was created for. We are all the happiest when we are doing what we were created to do. It's the same feeling a cheetah gets when it's running at lightning speed, a fish is swimming, or a bird in the air is flying. Notice how graceful and natural these animals look when they are doing what they are created to do. Also, notice that God has equipped them with the capabilities to be successful for what they were created to do. When your wife asks, "How can I help?" you can tell her! Don't try to do everything on your own. As men, we like to think that we should take on everything on our own to take the weight off the women. That is not how God intends for it to be. He knows you can't handle everything by yourself. That is why He created help! He sent help in the form of a woman. Not only does your wife want to help you, but she also actually *needs* to, as she will be the happiest operating with the unique God-given skills and capabilities He created her with.

# CHAPTER 16

# Security: Perfect Love Casts Out All Fear

Most people know about Abraham Maslow's hierarchy of needs. It's a ranking of what he theorizes drives every human being, starting from our most basic physical needs of food, water, and shelter, to psychological needs of self-esteem and relationships, to self-fulfillment needs of reaching one's full potential. As I look at his hierarchy of needs, what sticks out to me is that security seems like it is needed in every phase.

It would be no different for your wife. She needs to have a feeling of security at every stage. Maslow's pyramid consists of three tiers. The bottom tier includes physical needs and safety needs. Your wife needs to feel secure that her basic physical needs of food, water, shelter, and rest will always be provided. Not knowing if she will have a roof over her head because the mortgage is behind is not a secure feeling.

Tier one also includes the need to feel secure from danger and to feel safe. Your wife needs to feel confident that you will protect her, that being with you means she is always in a safe environment. This tier speaks of safety from more of a standpoint of physical harm.

The next tier on Maslow's pyramid is psychological needs. This includes self-esteem, personal accomplishments, intimacy, and belongingness. She needs to feel secure that she can be her true self around you. She needs to feel secure that you are not jealous of her accomplishments. She needs to feel secure in the relationship you have with each other, as well as her other relationships outside the marriage with friends and family. She shouldn't be fearful or doubting that you support her emotionally.

The last tier is self-fulfillment. Your wife should be secure and know that you support her in reaching her full potential and being all that God created her to be. The Bible says that perfect (or mature) understanding, comprehension, and knowledge of how much you are loved will eliminate these fears. In other words, the more she knows you love her, the more secure she will be. This security will penetrate and permeate into all areas. Every woman is different. There are different love languages. Love is received and perceived in different ways. Talk to your wife, and seek God in how to accurately express love to her so that fears decrease and a feeling of security reigns.

# CHAPTER 17

# Emotional Intelligence

*Increase your vocabulary because articulation is key.*

Men like to see. Women like to hear. Women are extremely capable of expressing their emotions, which isn't the case for most men. While it may not come as easily for a man to be emotionally expressive, it doesn't mean it's not needed. In fact, your wife needs to feel emotionally connected with you; she needs to hear what is on your mind and in your heart. Not saying anything does not nurture a feeling of security. It creates distance and does the exact opposite.

Let's face it—men are humans, too, which means we come programmed with emotions just as women do. Our struggle tends to lie in our not knowing exactly how to articulate them. It could have also come from the adage that was ingrained in us as boys: men should just suck it up, and big boys don't cry. Having been a product of this "philosophy," over the years, I've found that getting in touch with my emotions is continuous work and must be intentional. I must ask myself how I am feeling, why I am feeling a particular way, and then work to find the words to correctly communicate my emotions. What I learned is communication is key. Even better, clear and precise communication is key. Learning how to effectively communicate your thoughts and feelings is not something that's good to do; rather, it's a must. Your wife needs to hear it. If you don't have the words at that moment, it's fine to communicate just that, but when you do find the words, come back and speak to her.

The Bible provides several great points of reference about men sharing their emotions. As previously discussed, David was not only a warrior, but he was also a great king. He fought many battles and was as tough as they come, yet we see in the many psalms that David wrote that he was also able to express his deepest emotions. Pick any psalm and you will see firsthand David articulating what he's feeling; in fact, he's quite vulnerable. The book Song of Solomon is written in a similar manner; Solomon is pouring out his heart's love for a woman. An example is shared in the next chapter. Both David and Solomon are great examples of how we can communicate our truest emotions.

# CHAPTER 18

# Fight for Your Love

A woman needs to see that you are willing to fight for her love. The root of this is not jealousy from fear, but passion. In the book Song of Solomon 8:6 , it speaks of a "Love that is strong as death, and jealousy as cruel as the grave." And in 2 Corinthians 11:2 , it says, "For I am jealous over you with godly jealousy for I have espoused you to one husband, that I may present you as a chaste virgin to Christ."

God is saying that He passionately loves us, so much so that He will fight for that love. In the previous scripture, God is saying that He has godly jealousy for his love for us and that there is a passionate love that He has designed to be expressed between two people. The next verse speaks of God not wanting anyone (or anything) to sneak its way into that relationship. He is willing to fight for our love. We should be the same way, not out of fear, but out of passion.

A thief only comes to steal what is valuable. So we should be ever mindful that attacks on relationships will come. There is a godly comfort that a wife will have in knowing that you value the precious love and relationship the two of you share and can see that you are willing to fight for it. Too much passiveness in the relationship could appear as if you don't care and would let anything or anyone come in and interfere. Don't let this be the case. Be willing to fight for what is yours. She needs to see it and know it.

# CHAPTER 19

# Continual Assurance

Have you ever noticed that, throughout life, sometimes it feels like God is no longer present? You wonder if He still sees you, if He still cares, or if He even still loves you. When you first got saved, maybe you can remember exactly how you felt and where you were, what the Lord brought you out of, and how loved you felt. As time goes by and the monotony of life wears on us, the days get mundane, and the exciting moments come less and less often. We can begin to wonder where God is. The fact of the matter is that He is still there loving us, He is still there protecting us, He is still there watching over us, and He is still there providing for us. We want to always feel God's presence, and we forget so quickly the last thing He has done for us.

In the Old Testament, even though God performed amazing acts of love like parting the Red Sea, raining down food from heaven, and bringing forth water from a rock in the desert, the children of Israel soon forgot about those mighty acts of love. This tells me that, unfortunately, our love tank dwindles extremely quickly, and we can have short memories. This is true with us as well as our wives. She needs continual assurance of your love, an ever-evolving and deeper understanding and comprehension of just how much you love her. The last act of love you did for her has gotten stale; she needs a *fresh* revelation of your love. Even though you might have told her you loved her yesterday, she needs to hear it again today. And even though you told her with your words today, she needs to see it by your actions.

I'm sure you blew her away last year with that amazing anniversary gift, but what are you going to do this year? As I said earlier, love is perceived in different ways. Everyone has a unique set of love languages. Whatever language speaks to your wife that "I love you," whether it be words of affirmation, gifts, acts of service, quality time, or physical touch, it needs to be "spoken" consistently. God tells us that his mercies are new every morning. Whatever amount of mercy is used up in his "mercy tank" at the end of the day, it gets renewed at the beginning of the next day. If we can imagine that our wives have a love tank that needs to be refilled every morning, we can get a better idea of why we need to constantly and consistently be pouring into her tank!

# CHAPTER 20

# Held to a Higher Standard

This next chapter is extremely important and, once realized, could eliminate many of the arguments and much of the bickering that often is prevalent in marriages. We all know that marriage takes two people working together toward one goal. It requires not only giving and taking, but also sacrifices from both parties involved. Oftentimes, arguments happen when one side feels like they are doing a whole lot more sacrificing than the other. It doesn't feel too pleasant when one person feels like the other is not willing to match their efforts. We want someone who is accountable, and whatever personal standard we have set in our minds, we tend to hold our spouse to that exact same standard.

As a guy, I naturally spend a lot of time around my male friends, and one complaint I hear most is that men say their wives or girlfriends have a double standard. For example, they may say something like, "My wife gets on me if I leave one pair of socks lying on the floor, but she can leave two dresses, a coat, and three pairs of shoes lying around, and I can't say anything to her about it!"

Another guy yelps, "Yeah. When I'm searching for some food out of the fridge, if I leave the door open for one second too long, my wife barks at me to close the fridge door because 'You're letting all the cold air out, and the food's gonna spoil!' But she's looking for something in there for five minutes. As long as it's her looking, *then* it's OK." Every guy has his own story and example, and each man proceeds to share his own story, each trying to top the other with how much more ridiculous his example is than the next. Let's take a second to look at this whole double standard issue. I asked the Lord about this.

We are called to "love our wives as Christ loved the Church." How many times have you told the Lord that you're going to do something and then didn't do it? Maybe you said you're sorry, and maybe you didn't, but you automatically expected him to forgive you and kept moving right along. Yet if the Lord tells us something, and it doesn't happen quickly enough or on our time schedule, we go to the Lord infuriated and frustrated, attacking his character as if He didn't do what He said he would do. We can repeat the same bad action one hundred times and want the Lord to just show us grace and treat us the same way, but if we experience one bad trial in our life, we expect the Lord to have to answer for why he let us go through such a horrible atrocity. What if the Lord held us to the same standard that we try to hold him to? What if He pointed out to us everything we said we would do but fell short at—and then made us answer to him for it? What if He treated us differently because of it? Our relationship with the Lord would be entirely different if God chose to hold us to the exact same standard we try to hold him to. It sounds like we are the ones who have a double standard.

The truth is that Christ does not hold us to the same standard. Here is the reason why. He explained to me that He knows we are incapable of meeting it. Christ understands that we are tender and have weaknesses. He has compassion for us. Many times, our hearts are in the right place, but even when we try, we fall short. God is all-powerful. He cannot tell a lie, He can't go back on his word, He doesn't make mistakes, and He never falls short. It's impossible for us to operate at that standard. We are fallible. He is infallible. Christ holds himself to his own standard, and because He loves us, He has compassion for us. In doing so, He brings out the best in us.

Husbands, what does this mean for us? First of all, understand what I'm *not* saying. You are definitely not God, and you are just as imperfect and make just as many mistakes as any other human being. What I *am* saying is that because of the leadership position God has placed you in, you are to grant more patience and grace toward her than what is granted back to you in return. God is our perfect example of this. It does not mean that you let your wives just run all over you and do and say whatever they want. As I said earlier, good relationships call for both people to do their parts. There must always be constant communication and sacrifice on both parts. What this does mean is that you understand there is a higher standard you are held to. It means that just like Christ has compassion for us and our weaknesses, we are to do the same to our wives. It means we understand that there really is no such thing as a double standard.

Know that your wife, whether she realizes it or not, holds you to a higher standard than she holds herself. And guess what? The same can be said about us husbands. As you both work together and you learn to have compassion, rather than go tit for tat, then you will find it will bring about the best in her. The Bible says the Lord draws us with loving-kindness (Jer. 31:4), and he doesn't withhold his tender mercies. It's his love that causes us to willingly want to do better and try harder, not him getting on us and pointing out our faults.

Erase the myth of the double standard and begin to draw the best out of her with your mercy and kindness!

Romans 10:9-10 "states that if you confess with your mouth the Lord Jesus, and shall believe in your heart that God has raised him from the dead, you shall be saved. For with the heart man believes unto right-iousness; and with the mouth confession is made unto salvation." A great portion of this book speaks about having a personal relationship with Jesus Christ. If you currently don't have a relationship with Christ and would like to start one today you can pray a simple prayer and ask him to come into your heart.

Example: Lord Jesus, I believe that you died for me, I desire to get to know you personally. Come into my heart and reveal yourself to me. Amen